Wᴏʀʟᴅ Wᴀʀ II v
losing vision in ...
fers from macular degeneration, a progressive
illness that causes blindness. A drug could slow
the deterioration, but the government refuses
to pay for it. Why? He's not blind enough.
With his left eye spared so far, a government
panel has denied funding the pharmaceutical
even though his doctor feels it's needed.

No one doubts that Mr. Tagg is suffering. No
one denies that medications would help him.
The issue is cost. Mr. Tagg, frankly, isn't worth
it, according to a government bureaucracy
charged with making the funding decision.

Mr. Tagg isn't alone. This government panel
has considered other drugs: a kidney cancer
drug, which is expensive but proven to extend
life; a new and lifesaving breast-cancer drug;
an Alzheimer's drug shown to slow the deterioration of the patient's mind. Each time, the
government panel has said *no*.

Is this the future of American health care,

with a group of well-meaning government bureaucrats standing between a doctor and a patient, determining – quite literally – who will live and who will die?

Well, it's the reality of health care in Britain, where a government committee decides which drugs are worth funding by considering the monetary value of a year of life and measuring it against the cost of the medication. For those who feel that the United Kingdom has nothing to do with the American debate over health reform, consider this: One of the core ideas of ObamaCare is to create a British-style government panel to steer treatment decisions on this side of the Atlantic.

Rationing by committee. It's one of the ideas that will radically transform American health care, leaving us with a shattered private insurance market and a huge government bureaucracy.

Look to Britain to see the result – mass protests against government rationing decisions and people waiting for the most basic care. See it in Canada, where the new president of the Canadian Medical Association has declared, "We all agree that the system is imploding, we all agree that things are more precarious than perhaps Canadians realize." See it across the Western world.

See it, and realize this: Americans deserve better.

* * *

On the trail, candidate Barack Obama offered modest, simple ideas to better the health-care system, such as bringing in electronic health records and cracking down on Medicare fraud. He emphasized that he believed in bipartisanship. He also made a single, reassuring promise: "First of all, if you've got health insurance, you like your doctors, you like your plan, you can keep your doctor, you can keep your plan. Nobody is talking about taking that away from you."

The year 2009 has been about passing 1,100-page bills without reading them because of the urgency; dumbing down health policy to cartoonish simplifications with miracle cures (prevention), easy choices (a blue pill and a red pill), and villains (insurance companies and doctors); and reworking one-sixth of the nation's economy with practically no discussion.

There are winners with these reforms: trial lawyers and lobbyists. And there will be one big group of losers: the American people. That's because the proposed reforms are dangerous to our health.

The basic problem is not just the hardball, Chicago-style political strategy employed or the promise-breaking challenge to the status quo. The problem with President Obama's health proposals rests in their very ideological underpinning: that only with a new, massive role for the federal government will we better American health care.

This approach has proven a failure in other countries, leading to the rationing of care and the lowering of standards. It will prove disastrous here – a public-policy malpractice.

* * *

The problem with President Obama's health proposals rests in their very ideological under-pinning: that only with a new, massive role for the federal government will we better American health care.

THE NIGHTMARE OF GOVERNMENT-RUN HEALTH CARE

Is Washington the answer to our woes? Some Americans look at our health-care system – the most private in the Western world – and ask: Shouldn't we follow the example of other countries by tampering with the market and expanding coverage?

I understand the government temptation. I was born and raised in Canada. I did my medical training north of the 49th parallel.

And I once believed that government health care was compassionate and equitable.

But I learned the truth in medical school. Everyone in Canada is covered by a "single payer" – the government – and Canadians wait for practically any important procedure, diagnostic test or specialist consultation in their government-run, taxpayer-funded system.

This reality struck home when a relative had difficulty walking. He was in chronic pain. His doctor suggested a referral to a neurologist; an MRI was necessary, perhaps followed by a referral to another specialist. The wait would have stretched to roughly a year. If surgery was needed, the wait would have been months more. Not wanting to wait at home in pain, he had the surgery in the U.S., at the Mayo Clinic, and he paid for it himself.

Such stories are all too common. Sylvia de Vries, an Ontario woman, had a 40-pound fluid-filled tumor removed from her abdomen by an American surgeon in 2006. Her Michigan doctor estimated that she was within weeks of dying, but she was still on a wait list to see a Canadian specialist. Ms. de Vries is much in the news because she asked the Ontario government to cover her expenses, arguing that they failed to provide the lifesaving care she needed. To date, her request has been denied with a bureaucratically cold, if perfect, answer: Prior to getting her lifesaving surgery, she didn't complete the necessary paperwork.

Wait times in Canada are especially routine for diagnostic tests and elective surgeries. According to the government's own statistics – almost surely an understatement – people wait and wait and wait. In Alberta, Canada's wealthiest province, 50 percent of outpatients waited *more* than 41 days for an MRI scan in 2008. In Saskatchewan, 10 percent of patients awaiting knee-replacement surgery waited 616 days *or longer* for care. In Nova Scotia, 50 percent of hip-replacement patients waited 201 days *or longer* for surgery. Wait times for these and other procedures don't factor in any wait to get a referral from a family doctor – and more than 4 million Canadians can't find a family doctor because of a national doctor shortage created by government cutbacks to medical schools in the 1990s. The situation is so dire that some townships hold lotteries, with winners gaining access to a family doc.

Many liberals pretend these problems don't exist, cherry-picking good-news statistics to deny them. But Canada's Supreme Court put the issue to rest in 2005 when it found "evidence that delays in the public health care system are widespread, and that in some cases, patients die as a result of waiting lists for public health care."

Don't blame Canada. Blame socialized health care, which produces rationed care wherever it appears. In Britain, the National Health Service helpfully posts online reports on its progress toward an improved wait-time target – the standard is that no one should have to wait *more* than four and a half months for care. Ireland's socialized system is no better. At the April 2009 meeting of the Irish Medical Organisation, one Irish family doctor spoke out, complaining that orthopedic, gynecological and neurological patients faced waits at "their worst level" in his 25 years of experience. One of his patients waited 32 months to see a specialist, prompting the doctor to coin the phrase "health apartheid."

It's not an accident that service is slower in rationed systems. The investment by private insurance and private health providers pays for 15 percent more nurses in the United States than in Canada, four times as many MRI scanners per capita and more preventative tests for common cancers. Americans are global leaders in medical research and development; Canadians struggle to find capital for their own projects (and total R&D spending is less than that of the M. D. Anderson Cancer Center).

Rationing affects access to care. Data from the Joint Canada/United States Survey of Health shows that Americans are more likely to be treated for chronic illnesses. This study also finds that Canadians are less likely to have had preventative diagnostic procedures, particularly evident in at-risk populations. The screening gap: They are more than 15 percent less likely to have ever had a mammogram;

10 percent less likely to have had a Pap smear; 30 percent less likely to have had a PSA test; and more than 20 percent less likely to have ever had a colonoscopy. In a paper for the *Forum for Health Economics & Policy*, economists June O'Neill and David O'Neill argue that the low-income people in this socialized system are actually *less* healthy, relative to wealthier citizens, than their American counterparts.

The Canadian experience is hardly unique. Cancer data is collected across the Western world. A broad cancer review of Europe and the United States, published in September 2007 in *The Lancet Oncology*, considers five-year outcomes. For the 16 types of cancer examined in that paper, American men have a five-year survival rate of 66 percent, compared with only 47 percent for European men. In Europe, only Sweden has an overall survival rate of more than 60 percent. American women have a 63 percent chance of living at least five years after a cancer diagnosis, compared with 56 percent for European women; only five European countries have an overall survival rate of more than 60 percent.

Let's be clear. In countries like Canada, the approach to health care has not been reengineered. Primary care doesn't focus on wellness; chronic disease management is not more sophisticated than anything found in the United States. Rather, governments have simply rationed care, restricting the supply of providers, diagnostics and new drugs, and leaving people to suffer and, in the words of the Canadian Supreme Court justices, sometimes die.

Still, some argue that countries with government-run health care have found a way to tame the health-inflation problem. They claim that while costs spiral up in the U.S., these countries are doing better.

Actually, they aren't. Government-managed health-care systems are facing the same problems with health inflation. Yes, that's right – the cost of health care in socialized-care countries like France, Canada and Ireland is growing at roughly the same rate as in the United States. Between 2000 and 2006, the OECD average real annual growth rate for health spending was 4.9 percent; the U.S. rate was 4.95 percent. Despite the rationing and central government control, these countries haven't stopped the trend of rising costs.

Here, then, is the irony: From the White House to Capitol Hill, our leaders are looking abroad for ideas, as evidenced by the core ideas of ObamaCare.

ObamaCare: Government Health Care on the Installment Plan

President Obama insists that health-care reform is urgently needed to balance future federal budgets, yet his plan is to expand public programs – a major cause of future deficits in the first place. It's one of many contradictions as the White House seeks to "bend the curve" of health-care inflation but spend billions, possibly trillions, more.

What is the justification for ObamaCare? For decades, Democrats have hoped to deliver health coverage to every American. To achieve that, ObamaCare aims to subsidize health insurance for the uninsured. Without those subsidies, Congress cannot fairly pass a law requiring all Americans to buy health insurance. Without such a law, the president cannot claim to have health coverage for every American. When subsidies for insurance are added to the rising cost of existing taxpayer-funded health programs, America is adding jet fuel to the fire of public debts and deficits.

So the president also has another, competing goal: use health-care rationing and other measures to reduce overall health-care costs. The issue of cost was so central to the birth of

---

Democrats plan to fight inflation with the only weapon they trust: more government control.

ObamaCare, the president used the four-letter word "cost" 36 times in a recent press conference on health care. And Democrats plan to fight inflation with the only weapon they trust: more government control.

To achieve these goals, the president has repeatedly said it would make sense for him to create a single-payer, Canadian-style health-care system if he were starting from scratch. The president acknowledges this isn't possible because health care is a large part of the American economy, "and we're not suddenly just going to completely upend the system." Instead, Democratic leaders in Congress are designing a hybrid plan – a go-slow plan that acts as government health care, on the installment plan.

To guide Congress in this effort, President Obama offered three principles for health reform:

- Reduce the cost to government, consumers and the economy.

- Guarantee a choice of plans and doctors.

- Offer affordable coverage for all (universal coverage).

At face value, these principles sound fair. Read them another way, and these principles describe the benefits of the Canadian single-payer system as Democrats portray them.

To get as close to a single-payer system as possible, ObamaCare surrounds private and nonprofit health care with a wall of new government programs and regulations.

› To reduce the cost of Medicare and Medicaid, new bureaucracies in Washington will have the power to impose "cost-effective" health-care solutions – so the federal government can force your doctor to deliver cheaper care, just as government-run systems do. These edicts on coverage eventually could be imposed on private insurers.

› Most Americans are happy with their current coverage. As a result, ObamaCare "guarantees" that their plan will remain intact but changes how those plans are regulated, potentially making them financially unsustainable.

‣ To deliver affordable coverage for all, the ObamaCare plan includes a public insurance option. It will likely subsidize (directly and indirectly) subscribers to this public insurance plan, making private insurance less competitive than the public option.

Three controversial ideas come up again and again as the key components of ObamaCare.

1 · The Health-Insurance Exchange

American health insurance is more expensive because private insurers compete within state markets, not regional or national markets. The easiest way to encourage competition is to let the general public choose from competing private plans in a national market, just as federal employees do. To make this so-called national "Health Insurance Exchange" work, Congress is exploring new rules to increase the reliability and transparency of private insurance plans.

However, many of these new rules are likely to make health inflation worse, not better. Health-policy analysts call these regulations mandates. *Mandates* are the earmarks of the health-policy world. In the past, state law-makers added insurance mandates to various laws, forcing plans to cover specific services and providers.

Thanks to mandates, insurers in one state (New Mexico) must cover oriental medicine in every insurance policy. Two states (Washington and Minnesota) require coverage for "port wine stain elimination." Three states have mandates for athletic trainers. Twelve states force insurers to cover acupuncture. Fifteen states force insurers to cover in vitro fertilization. In these and hundreds of similar cases, insurance mandates distort prices upward to reward different political agendas – and consumers pay.

Consider Wisconsin and New York. New Yorkers pay $12,000 for a basic insurance plan that would cost $3,000 in Wisconsin. The difference? Wisconsin has 34 mandates. New York has 51. By one estimate, mandates and other health regulations drive up the cost of premiums by 20 to 50 percent.

The Health Insurance Exchange can bring

premium prices down only if insurers are allowed to compete in an open national marketplace. But now, Democrats in Congress are adding *federal* mandates to replace the state mandates. Politics could transform the Health Insurance Exchange into a rigged roulette wheel – rigged in favor of the new government-run insurance company.

2 · Public Option

President Obama and other Democrats insist that the only way to keep insurance companies "honest" is to create a public insurance, modeled after Medicare, to compete against them. This is the so-called "public option." Once the Health Insurance Exchange opens, Democrats don't believe the 240 or so private plans will represent enough choice for the American people. The president has so far insisted on one more choice – a government insurance, designed by Washington, added to the public coverage already offered through Medicare and Medicaid.

As far back as December 2008, a columnist

called the public option "a beautiful jewel" of health reform in the liberal *American Prospect* before the president had even announced his full support. In *The Washington Post* in June, liberal blogger Ezra Klein wrote that a "strong" public insurance option was "the single most recognizable marker for victory" in health-care reform (even as he admitted that there were three very different "flavors" of public option on the table). Apparently, it doesn't matter if the public option is competitive, affordable or effective. All that matters is that there be a new program run by the government. After months of hype, it's no surprise that almost three-quarters of Americans polled said it couldn't hurt to have the choice of a public health-insurance plan – even if less than a third actually planned to use it.

But it *can* hurt to have the choice, and it can hurt badly. A new public insurance would be backed by the faith and credit of the United States taxpayer and supported by a Congress with a vested interest in stacking the "honest" competition. Indeed, the House bill would exempt the public plan from state taxes and regulations, require minimal capitalization and establish Medicare-style rates of paying providers. Over time, the public plan – able to offer artificially low premiums compared with taxed, regulated, capitalized and non-price-controlled private plans – would be a magnet for enrollment and accomplish what it has done in other countries: crowd out private insurance, reduce private investment, restrain national medical capacity and shift more health decisions into the hands of government-appointed bureaucrats.

That's the most likely scenario. The Congressional Budget Office estimates that about 15 million Americans would sign up for the public plan. The Lewin Group, a well-regarded consulting firm, has suggested that as many as 114 million Americans could shift from private to public coverage. Which estimate is more accurate? The difference rests with the assumptions (the extent of price controls, for example). In truth, it's a problem either way.

If the public option is popular, then the benefits of private health investment will gradually be wiped out as government-run insurance dominates the marketplace – hence the criticism that the public option is a "Trojan horse" for socialized health insurance. But suppose the public option fails? If so, Washington will have needlessly created new laws, new regulations and new bureaucracy to duplicate services while helping only a small number of Americans.

Liberal Democrats already have introduced tough new laws to ban insurance cancellations, make insurance plans more portable between jobs and cities and force insurers to sell policies to Americans with preexisting conditions. A public option has nothing to do with keeping insurers honest and everything to do with expanding the government's direct influence over doctors, clinics and patients.

3 · Rationing by Committee

Recently, Democratic leaders added a new feature to the ObamaCare plan. It's called the

Independent Medicare Advisory Council, or IMAC. Obama budget czar Peter Orszag believes the council can use a "comparative effectiveness analysis" to change how doctors prescribe treatments in America, restraining health-care inflation by imposing cost-cutting decisions on doctors. IMAC will have the power to reject treatments, devices or drugs for Medicare coverage unless specifically vetoed by Congress or the president. In theory, IMAC's guidance on Medicare costs will then be adopted by other government agencies and the private sector.

Democrats insist that they don't want British or Canadian-style health care. But we've seen a version of IMAC at work in Britain. In the U.K., the rationing committee is called the National Institute for Health and Clinical Excellence, or NICE.

NICE has not lived up to its name. The institute spent two years restricting a drug to treat blindness, claiming patients could get by with just one working eye. NICE rejected a life-extending kidney cancer drug even after certifying its effectiveness, arguing that saying yes would force budget cuts elsewhere in the government-run system. And while Democrats insist they don't want Canadian health care, there is a Canadian counterpart to IMAC, the secretive Common Drug Review, or CDR. For the record, the CDR has rejected several orphan drugs without public debate, even though these drugs are often the only treatment for rare diseases.

The problem with NICE is that "comparative effectiveness" has never really been about improving effectiveness; it's always been about reducing cost. With quality of care compromised, British courts and grassroots campaigns have repeatedly forced NICE to reconsider its decisions. NICE did little to stop Britain's health-care inflation, with annual rates besting general inflation by as much as 7 percent at points this decade. Even with central management by bureaucrats in London, British health-care inflation is outpacing American health-care inflation.

Critics of American insurance companies

often attack the practice of "rescission" – the cancellation of an insurance policy that a subscriber is already paying for. Sometimes, policies are canceled because the company alleges fraud on the part of the patient. In other cases, insurance is revoked because of a preexisting condition or a dispute over portability. Whatever the cause, the fear of losing health coverage that's already been bought just when it's needed most is one of the most politically controversial features of the American health-care system.

Americans will likely be happy to learn that ObamaCare bans rescission. But while it bans *private* rescission with one hand, it creates *government* rescission with the other. Rescission puts patients in limbo, one patient at a time. IMAC rationing will do the same, but for millions of patients at a time. And now, President Obama's advisers are calling IMAC "the most important game-changer" in their plan to cut health-care costs.

* * *

The ObamaCare proposals remain a work in progress as the White House furiously polls and hones its message. It's possible that, by press time, some of these proposals will be watered down – for example, the Medicare-style public plan could instead be some type of not-for-profit co-op program.

But be mindful of this: They are just dressing up government health care in a new set of clothes. Federally controlled, federally staffed, federally managed and federally financed – the co-op looks like a new version of their old idea: the public option. And we know their ultimate goal.

More Washington, Less Care

The president insists that he wants to preserve what's best about the American system. His plan, however, does the opposite.

The White House points to the Mayo Clinic and the Cleveland Clinic as examples for American health providers to follow. But neither of these efficient, quality-care clinics was

The president insists that he wants to preserve what's best about the American system. His plan, however, does the opposite.

created by a Washington committee. Neither needed a "public option" to keep it honest. In socialized health systems like Canada's, innovative delivery models violate national or provincial policies. To protect the "equality" of the government-run system in Canada, innovative new care models (like stand-alone private MRI clinics) are banned in some provinces.

Of course, it's easy to attack Washington, government-run care and waiting lists in other countries. It's easy – and right – to complain that the president has tried to do too much, too quickly and with too much government. Critics from both parties have stalled the president's agenda because of those criticisms.

But once all of the smoke clears, if Obama-

Care disappeared tomorrow, Americans would still face rising premiums, health-care inflation and a health system that rewards unhealthy behavior. The president has attacked his critics as "defenders of the status quo," insisting critics must provide a better answer. What, then, should be done to reform American health care?

WHAT'S RIGHT, WHAT'S WRONG, AND WHAT'S TO BE DONE

American medicine has never been better, yet millions are dissatisfied with American health care. This is the paradox that lies at the heart of the debate.

We are surrounded by medical miracles. Cardiac care has been revolutionized in only a few short years; death due to cardiac disease has fallen by nearly two-thirds in the past five decades. Polio is confined to the history books. Childhood leukemia, once a death sentence, is curable. Depression and mental illnesses are treatable.

Americans are at the forefront of this medical revolution. People from all over the world seek American medicine when they need help. And American excellence isn't confined to the hospital or the clinic. When 300 internists were asked to rank major medical innovations in a survey for the journal *Health Affairs*, eight of the top 10 they ranked were developed, in whole or in part, in the United States. American scientists map the genome, produce cutting-edge biotech drugs and develop surgical procedures for fetuses – interventions before birth itself.

Yet while the quality of American medicine has never been better, angst over American health care has never been greater.

In newspapers, on the radio and in the blogs, commentators describe a system in "crisis." The unsustainability of Medicare. The number of uninsured. The rising costs. The uneven quality. Health-care reform is the biggest domestic issue of this year because people are anxious.

They wonder: Are we getting value for

money? American health care seems feverishly expensive. Health-insurance premiums have roughly doubled since 2000 – but would even the slickest Washington lobbyist claim that the care is twice as good?

The constant, unrelenting rise in costs, year after year, is a source of much angst. It has hit middle America in the pocketbook. Between 2000 and 2006, the earnings of the median American worker stagnated, despite annual wage increases, because insurance premiums swallowed up the money. Rising health costs caused a recession for millions of working Americans before the housing bubble burst and the Dow plunged.

American health care, in other words, needs reform. It should start with the reform of health insurance – but primarily with competition, not standardization and regulation. Consumer power, not government power, will lower costs and increase options. And we need to emphasize health, not just health care. These are the three principles for meaningful reform. (For a more detailed discussion of the

Consumer power, not government power, will lower costs and increase options.

flaw of American health care and how to apply these principles, please see the Afterword.)

But ObamaCare is not about building on what's right and addressing the challenges. It's a government takeover.

Yes, there are too many uninsured Americans, but insurance reform that would eventually see tens of millions of Americans shifted to a public program is not the answer. Yes, costs are rising, but rationing by bureaucracy is not the answer. Yes, more choices are needed, but a rigidly regulated health-insurance exchange designed to change everyone's plans is not the answer.

The history of medicine is filled with examples of well-meaning doctors who get the diagnosis right but end up administering a treatment worse than the disease. ObamaCare stands as much chance of success as bleeding an elderly man with chest pain.

* * *

AFTERWORD: HOW TO CURE AMERICAN HEALTH CARE

Why is American health care so feverishly expensive? Because it's so cheap.

In other sectors of the economy, costs fall with time. Think of agriculture or transportation – areas that, like health care, have been transformed by technology and innovation. But the advancement of medical science has, curiously, not followed the trend. Indeed, progress means *greater* expense. Year after year, health spending rises, from 5 percent of GDP in 1960 to more than triple that today.

The central problem is the way Americans pay for their care. Rather than paying directly, most people get their health insurance from their employers. Someone else foots the bill. Our employers don't pay directly for other basic needs, like food, clothing or shelter. So how did this odd financing arrangement develop for health care? The answer can be found in the tax code.

The biggest event to shape American health insurance occurred on October 26, 1943. Given the importance of that date, some might think that Congress passed a major piece of legislation or that the Supreme Court decided a landmark case. Actually, the date marks a special ruling on health benefits by the Internal Revenue Service declaring that employees would not be taxed on premiums paid on their behalf by their employers.

The IRS didn't make this ruling out of the blue. Two years earlier, in 1941, the Roosevelt administration had imposed wage and price controls as part of the war effort. The effects of price controls are well-remembered – for instance, a black market for gasoline quickly developed. Wage controls also produced unintended consequences as employers sought ways to provide workers with competitive salaries without violating the law. Across

America, employers found their answer in health benefits. The IRS ruling legitimized the practice.

Today, most Americans receive their health insurance through their employers. No wonder – historically, it has made sense for firms to offer health benefits, and lots of them do. If an employer offers his employee a raise of $1,000 a month, the employee will probably take home $600 after income and payroll tax. But if the employer offers $1,000 more of health benefits, the employee gets every dollar's worth. It's not surprising, then, that many company plans offer sunglasses, massage therapy and marital counseling. These aren't essential ingredients for wellness; they represent disguised income.

Public insurances – Medicare and Medicaid – also were shaped by the 1940s. It was then that the British conceived and designed their National Health Service, a zero-dollar deductible insurance. It took the United States a couple of decades to implement its own public coverage, with principles based on the

British experience. Thus, for the most part, America's elderly and poor also pay little out of pocket for covered health services.

The resulting accidental system is fraught with problems. For one thing, health insurance covers just about everything. Usually, insurance covers people for rare and unforeseen events. Car insurance, for example, helps in the event of a major accident, but not for filling the car with gas after a long Sunday drive or replacing worn brake pads. In contrast, health insurance covers annual physical exams and routine blood work. Indeed, between private and public coverage, Americans are overinsured, paying pennies on the dollar. Today, Americans pay directly just 13 cents on every health-care dollar.

The implications for cost were quite direct. As Nelson Sabatini, twice Maryland's secretary of Health and Mental Hygiene, reflected, "Using health care in this country is like shopping with someone else's credit card." That is the core economic problem with American health care.

ObamaCare doesn't address this problem. If anything, with a round of new subsidies, it will make it worse.

* * *

What we need instead is a made-in-America solution to our health-care woes.

Americans rely on individual choice and competition as organizing principles for five-sixths of the economy. In those areas, prices fall, technology advances, quality increases. Yet with health care, the United States has taken a different approach. Between public and private coverage, America's health-care system is built on a 1940s idea of third-party payment.

The regulatory framework isn't modern either: The Food and Drug Administration was created a century ago, and its scope dramatically expanded about 50 years ago. America needs 21st-century medicine delivered by a modern system. What we have is a government infrastructure that dates back to the era when penicillin was considered experimental, FDR was the president and the total population of the United States was just 100 million. A fresh approach is needed.

Here are 10 reforms for a better health-care system and a healthier nation.

1. *Make health insurance more like other types of insurance.*

You don't buy car insurance to cover you for gas and tune-ups or home insurance for a quick paint job, but health insurance includes everything from a physical to cancer care – it covers too much. Health savings accounts, which passed as part of the Medicare reforms of 2003, were an important first step, separating smaller expenses from the costs of catastrophic events. However, the legislation is overly rigid. Congress must expand and revise the structure of health savings accounts.

2. *Foster competition.*

American health care is the most regulated sector of the economy. The result? A health-insurance policy for a 30-year-old man costs four times more in New York than in neighboring Connecticut because of the multitude of regulations in the Empire State. Americans can shop out of state for a mortgage; they should be able to do so for health insurance. And greater competition isn't simply needed at the insurance level.

3. *Make it as easy as possible for people to get coverage.*

It's difficult for small businesses to make health-insurance decisions for their employees. Washington should make things easier. Allowing association health plans – where different businesses can work together to buy insurance – would be important. And health-insurance exchanges also could be useful, but they should be implemented at the state level (with Congress's encouragement).

4. *Directly help the uninsured.*

While the issue of the uninsured is much more complicated than typically presented – roughly 9 million uninsured are noncitizens and 10 million uninsured have the income for insurance but opt not to buy – some Americans do fall through the cracks. Presently, the federal government spends billions on uncompensated care, funding hospitals. That money should be turned over to the states to let them experiment with directly helping the uninsured, for example, through voucher programs for private insurance. States could also use the money to help establish high-risk pools for the chronically ill.

5. *Reform Medicaid, using welfare reform as the template.*

Like the old Aid to Families with Dependent Children, Medicaid is expensive and not very good. Even *The New York Times* has acknowledged that the program is plagued by "waste, fraud, and abuse." Part of the problem stems from the fact that the program is shared between federal and state government – and is owned by neither. Congress should fund Medicaid with block grants to the states and let them innovate.

6. Revisit Medicare.

With an aging population, Medicare is quickly becoming unaffordable. In the late 1990s, a bipartisan commission approved a reasonable starting point for Medicare: junking the price controls and using the Federal Employees Health Benefits Plan as a model to give elderly Americans a choice among competing private plans. The time is right to experiment with this idea.

7. Increase transparency.

American health care largely remains a black box, with limited information available to people regarding cost and quality. Washington should promote efforts that increase transparency, allowing patients to get better information on both the cost and quality of health services. Some of these initiatives will come from the public sector – in New Jersey, as an example, the state publishes data on post-cardiac surgery outcomes. The federal government can also allow private and not-for-profit organizations to help patients by releasing more Medicare data.

8. *Address prescription drug prices by pruning the size and scope of the FDA.*

It costs nearly a billion dollars for a prescription drug to reach the market, and roughly 40 percent of that sum is due to the FDA's safety requirements. This is effectively a massive tax on pharmaceuticals. With new technology and focus, it should be possible to update the FDA, its structure and its mandate.

9. *End defensive medicine.*

By one estimate, $30 billion a year is spent on medical malpractice suits. But the hidden cost is much higher, as physicians often order tests and practice defensive medicine with trial lawyers in mind, not their patients' interests, pushing up the cost of care by more than $100 billion a year. Capping noneconomic damages – thereby allowing wronged patients to receive compensation, but not absurdly large amounts – would be reasonable, a reform already seen in states like Texas and California. But Washington should go further, moving emotional malpractice cases to specialized, expert-driven courts.

10. Better America's health.

Americans are unhealthy. Obesity, once a rarity, affects one in four adults. Much has to do with the choices we make, including diet and exercise. There is no simple solution, but several measures are needed. The federal government should stop subsidizing certain foods. Health plans should be designed to promote healthier choices; yet, ironically, federal legislation often limits these efforts – Washington should review and reverse such limitations.

A CASE STUDY IN SUCCESS

Safeway is America's third-largest grocery chain, with more than 200,000 employees. Like many large corporations, Safeway self-insures its health expenses. Safeway also needs a large pool of workers for tasks as diverse as inventory, customer service and logistics management – so cherry-picking only the healthiest insurance prospects is not an option.

To attack the threat of rising health-care costs, Safeway created a Healthy Measures program for its nonunion work force (a majority of Safeway employees aren't unionized). The company targets smoking, weight, blood pressure and unhealthy cholesterol, setting targets for healthy performance. These are all areas where people can improve their health with simple, affordable behavior choices: Don't smoke, watch your salt intake, walk more, eat a little better, and you'll be well on your way to the Healthy Measures targets. Healthier employees don't just keep payroll and insurance costs down for everyone – they also receive cash incentives as a reward.

The result: Four years into the pilot project, Safeway has transformed its health-insurance balance sheet, producing a net-zero percent (0%) gain in per-employee health insurance costs. In the same period, comparable companies saw their costs rise by an average of almost 40 percent.

The president is in a hurry to pass health-care legislation to meet a self-imposed deadline. But Congress is moving at a slower pace. People will have a chance to voice their opinions. It might take years to fill in the details, so there will be time to push for improvements and alternatives.

If you're not on the record with your views, be sure to contact your senator or your congressman. Be polite: Health-care finance is complicated, and even the worst ideas often come from people with the best of intentions. And don't forget to make your views known to your state representatives. States are critical to the delivery of health care, and they have been neglected in this year's health-care debate by ObamaCare supporters and opponents alike.

American health care needs to be reformed. But we are at a crossroads. Some want to expand Washington's reach, pushing American health care down the road that countries like Britain and Canada have traveled. There is an alternative. Five-sixths of the economy is based on individual choice and competition.

Is there really any question what way we should head?

First American edition published in 2009 by Encounter Books, an activity of Encounter for Culture and Education, Inc., a nonprofit, tax exempt corporation. Encounter Books website address: *www.encounterbooks.com*

Manufactured in the United States and printed on acid-free paper. The paper used in this publication meets the minimum requirements of ANSI/NISO Z39.48-1992 (R 1997) (*Permanence of Paper*).

FIRST AMERICAN EDITION

LIBRARY OF CONGRESS CATALOGING-IN-PUBLICATION DATA

Gratzer, David.
Why Obama's government takeover of health care will be a disaster / by David Gratzer.
p.   cm.
ISBN-13: 978-1-59403-460-2 (pbk. : alk. paper)
ISBN-10: 1-59403-460-5 (pbk. : alk. paper)
1. Health care reform—United States. I. Title.
RA395.A3G715 2010
362.10973'0905—dc22
2009033854

10 9 8 7 6 5 4 3 2 1